Comets and Meteors

Mason Crest
450 Parkway Drive, Suite D
Broomall, PA 19008
www.masoncrest.com

Printed and bound in the United States of America.

First printing
9 8 7 6 5 4 3 2 1
Series ISBN: 978-1-4222-3547-8
ISBN: 978-1-4222-3548-5
E-book ISBN: 978-1-4222-8368-4

Library of Congress Cataloging-in-Publication Data on file with the publisher.

THE SOLAR SYSTEM

Comets and Meteors • Far Planets • Giant Planets • Near Planets
Our Home Planet • Space Exploration • The Sun

KEY ICONS TO LOOK FOR:

 EDUCATIONAL VIDEOS: Readers can view videos by scanning our QR codes, providing them with additional educational content to supplement the text. Examples include news coverage, moments in history, speeches, iconic sports moments and much more!

 WORDS TO UNDERSTAND: These words with their easy-to-understand definitions will increase the reader's understanding of the text while building vocabulary skills.

Contents

Introduction

Nearly every time you go stargazing, you will see little streaks of light in the sky. It looks as if some of the stars are shooting off to another part of the heavens, or falling toward the ground. That is why people call these streaks **shooting stars** or falling stars. But their proper name is **meteors**. Meteors are specks of matter from space burning up as they pass through the **atmosphere**.

These specks are some of the many lumps and bits of matter that are found in the space between the **planets**. Sometimes bigger lumps pass through the night sky and are lit up by the Sun. We see them as **comets**, with a glowing **head** and a long tail fanning out behind. There are also larger lumps still that we can't see, orbiting in the space between Mars and Jupiter. These are the **asteroids**. It's pretty crowded out there in the **Solar System**!

Night Sky Spectaculars

Meteors and comets are among the most exciting sights in the night sky.

Usually, the changes that take place in the night sky occur gradually. The **constellations**, or star patterns, appear and disappear as the months go by. The planets wander slowly against the background of stars.

But meteors and comets appear and disappear suddenly. Meteors come and go in seconds. And they may be seen in any part of the sky. Exceptionally bright meteors may glow all the colors of the rainbow and may even explode. We call them **fireballs**.

Famed physicist Stephen Hawking describes how the Solar System was formed.

Catching comets

Comets take longer to come and go. These days astronomers are not surprised when comets appear because they have usually spotted them in telescopes months before. Most comets pass through the heavens quickly—you can easily notice them changing position among the stars night by night.

Not all comets are bright enough to see with the naked eye. In fact, bright comets are quite rare. But stargazers in the late 1990s were fortunate to see very bright comets for two years running. They were Hyakutake in 1996 and Hale-Bopp in 1997. They both became brighter than all but the brightest stars and were truly spectacular.

◁ This spectacular comet of 1997, Hale-Bopp, hangs in the western sky just after sunset. It was one of the brightest comets of the twentieth century, as bright as the brightest stars.

Taking photographs

You can take photographs of meteors
and bright comets with most cameras.
They must have a time setting. This will let
you keep the camera shutter open for as
long as you want.

You will also need two other pieces
of equipment, a tripod and a cable
shutter release. The tripod helps hold the
camera steady, while the cable release
stops you jogging it when you open and
close the shutter. If you use a film camera,
choose a fast film, perhaps ISO 400.

> ▷ Halley's famous
> comet, pictured on
> its last return,
> in 1985-86.

To photograph a
bright comet, point
the camera at the
comet and keep the
shutter open for about
a minute. If you keep it
open for much longer,
the stars in the picture
will show up as little
trails as they move.

Hit or miss

Photographing
meteors is more hit
and miss, especially
with digital cameras,
because meteors
can appear in any
direction. The best thing to do is to point
the camera to different parts of the sky in
turn, keeping the shutter open for, say, an
hour or so each time. When the film is
developed, you may be lucky to find
meteor streaks on it—or you may
not! Nevertheless, you will have
some nice star trails.

◁ An astronomer
photographing Comet
Brooks in 1993 also
captured a fiery
meteor trail.

Stars of Ill Omen

Most ancient peoples believed comets brought death and destruction.

People who lived long ago knew very little about their world. And they knew even less about the heavenly bodies. But they had a feeling that their lives were somehow ruled by what happened in the heavens. This belief became known as astrology.

When comets suddenly appeared without warning in the sky, people became scared. It seemed a very bad sign. This belief, that comets were bad news, lasted for thousands of years.

Chinese broom stars

As early as the 600s BC, Chinese writers said that comets were, "vile stars." They caused emperors to die, uprisings among the people, floods, drought, and diseases. The Chinese were very skilled observers of the heavens, and seemed particularly interested in comets. Their earliest records of comets date as far back as 1400 BC.

The ancient Chinese called comets broom stars, thinking that their tails looked like the bristles on a broom.

Other peoples have called them stars with feathers and hair stars. This idea is echoed in the modern word comet, which comes from the Greek word **coma**, meaning hair.

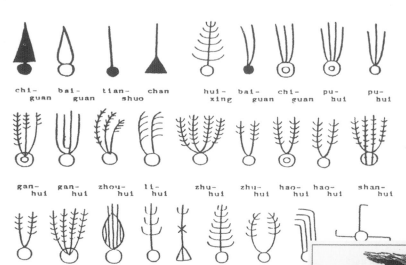

△ Ancient Chinese astronomers recorded many kinds of comets. These sketches are based on drawings dating back to 186 BC.

▷ The brilliant 1664 comet, as seen at Nuremberg, Germany.

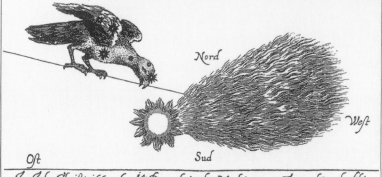

More bad news

Comets have been blamed for all kinds of disasters. Roman writers said they caused wars. In the Middle Ages, it was said that comets always appeared when kings and princes died.

This certainly proved true in 1066, when a comet appeared in the sky at the time of the Battle of Hastings. King Harold and the English army were fighting the invading Norman army led by William the Conqueror. The English lost the battle after Harold was killed. The 1066 comet later proved to be a regular visitor to Earth's skies. It is now known as Halley's Comet.

△ The Bayeux tapestry shows the comet of 1066 above King Harold on the throne of England.

△ Edmond Halley realized that some comets visit our skies regularly.

Epidemics from space
Some astronomers have suggested that comets carry tiny primitive organisms (life forms), such as bacteria and viruses. As they pass near to the Sun, the microorganisms drift into space. In time they enter the Earth's atmosphere and cause worldwide epidemics, such as influenza.

The fall of the Aztecs

In Mexico in 1519, Montezuma, the Aztec king, saw two brilliant comets. He took this as a sign that the white-bearded god Quetzalcoatl was coming. Not long after, the bearded Hernan Cortés arrived with his Spanish soldiers. Thinking that Cortés was the god, Montezuma welcomed him. But, within a short time, the Spaniards had all but wiped out the Aztec civilization.

Heads and Tails

A bright comet is a spectacular sight. Its bright head looks like a flaming arrow pointing towards the Sun. Its tail fanning out behind stretches for millions of miles across the starry sky.

But what exactly is a comet? Mostly it is a great cloud of gas and dust, like the smog that forms in polluted cities on Earth. The cloud is lit up by sunlight and shows up brilliantly against the blackness of space.

Only deep inside the comet's head is there a solid bit, called the **nucleus.** Compared with the size of the whole comet, the nucleus is tiny. In most comets, it is only between about a mile or two across. The bright 1997 comet Hale-Bopp was unusual in having an exceptionally big nucleus, maybe as big as 24 miles (40 km) across.

Dirty snowballs

The nucleus of a comet is often described as a dirty snowball, because it seems to be made up mainly of water ice and dust. When a comet enters the inner Solar System, the Sun's heat makes the ice on the surface of the comet evaporate, or turn to vapor (gas). The gas spurts out of the nucleus in jets, carrying dust with it. Large comets like Hale-Bopp give off vast amounts of gas and dust—as much as 1,000 tons of dust and 150 tons of gas every second.

The gas and dust form a cloud around the nucleus, hundreds of thousands of miles across. This cloud is the glowing head of the comet, or coma. The coma is surrounded by an even bigger cloud, made up of hydrogen atoms.

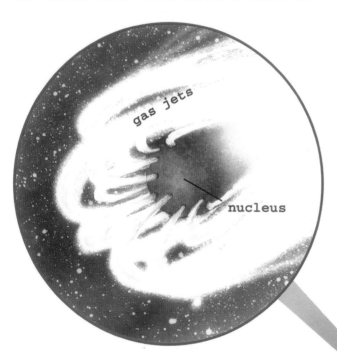

gas jets

nucleus

△ Jets of gas shoot out of the tiny nucleus of a comet, forming a huge glowing cloud around it. Sunlight forces the gas into a long, broad tail.

▷ Comet West, a striking sight in spring skies in March 1976. Here we see its two tails clearly—the blue one is the gas, or ion tail.

The hydrogen cloud is invisible in ordinary light, but shows up in pictures taken in ultraviolet light.

Telling tails

The most spectacular part of a comet is its **tail**, or rather tails, because most comets have two tails.

How do comets grow tails? Jets of gas and dust spurt out of the comet nucleus on the hottest side, which faces the Sun. As they spurt out, they come up against the **solar wind**. This is a stream of particles flowing out from the Sun. The wind sweeps the gas and dust backwards.

Soon two distinct tails develop, one made by the gas, one by the dust. The particles in the solar wind hit the gas particles and make them electrically charged. They become what are called ions, and start to glow. They form the gas, or ion tail. Sunlight pushes the dust particles into another tail, the **dust tail**.

◁ A false-color view of Halley's comet in 1986, showing different levels of brightness.

In from the Cold

Comets seem to appear suddenly in the heavens, and then brighten as they move towards the Sun. As they move away from the Sun, they fade and disappear from view. It is this sudden appearance and disappearance that frightened people in the past. But comets do not really suddenly appear and disappear. Like other bodies in the Solar System, they follow **orbits**, or paths through space as they travel around the Sun.

But for most of the time their orbits take comets away from the Sun into the dark depths of the Solar System. Little heat or light reaches them there, and so they remain frozen solid and invisible.

△ When first spotted, a comet looks like a glowing ball.

It is only when comets start to close in on the Sun that they begin to light up. They also start to melt and release their cloud of gas and dust and grow tails. With most comets this happens when they approach the orbit of Mars, 155 million miles (250 million km) away from the Sun. After they loop around the Sun and travel back into space, they disappear at about the same distance.

tails grow shorter

Sun

comet orbit

tails grow longer

△ Comet tails always point away from the Sun as the solar wind pushes them. Comets develop the longest tails when they get closest to the Sun.

Curving orbits

Comets have different kinds of orbits from the planets. The planets travel around the Sun in nearly circular orbits. They also travel in much the same plane (flat sheet) in space and in the same direction. And from the Earth, we see the planets move through the same part of the sky.

Comets could not be more different. They have all kinds of oval and curving orbits. They can appear and disappear anywhere in the sky and move in any direction.

▽ **This false-color picture shows Halley's comet in 1910.**

17:56 UT

Out of the clouds
Astronomers think that long—**period** comets come from a huge ring of icy bodies known as the Oort Cloud. It stretches from about 90 billion miles from the Sun to about 3 quadrillion miles, or nearly half-way to the nearest stars.

The long and the short

Some comets travel in orbits that bring them back near the Sun in quite a short time, or period. One, called Encke's Comet, returns every 3.3 years. Astronomers call it a periodical comet, and term it P/Encke. Halley's Comet P/Halley, returns to Earth's skies after every 76 years or so. In general, comets with return periods up to 200 years are called short-period comets.

Most bright comets that appear have not been recorded before and have long periods. They have wide, curving orbits that may not bring them back near the Sun for thousands of years. The 1997 comet Hale-Bopp will probably not return for 4,000 years; the 1974 comet Kohoutek, won't be back for 75,000 years.

◁ **The space probe SOHO spots two comets diving into the Sun. This happens when comets get too close.**

Edmond Halley's Comet

In January 1681, a brilliant comet blazed in Earth's skies. Among the many who watched it was an English astronomer named Edmond Halley. After another bright comet appeared the following year, he worked out its orbit. Then he checked its orbit with the orbits of other comets that had appeared in the past.

Halley found that comets that had appeared in 1607 and 1537 seemed to have similar orbits to the 1682 comet. He was convinced that these comets were one and the same, returning to Earth's skies about every 76 years. In 1705, he published a book about comets and predicted that the comet of 1682 would return in 1758.

Halley died in 1742. Sixteen years later, on Christmas night 1758, a German astronomer found the comet Halley had predicted. Since then, Edmond Halley's Comet has returned to Earth's skies three times, the most recent being in 1986. It will return next in 2061.

Target Halley

When Halley's Comet returned in 1986, it proved to be disappointing for most people. It was only just visible to the naked eye in certain parts of the world. But astronomers studied it closely in telescopes. And space scientists launched **probes** to spy on the comet from close quarters.

The most successful probe was *Giotto*, launched by the European Space Agency (ESA), which went closest to the comet. Russia sent two probes (*Vega 1* and *2*); so did Japan (*Sakigake and Suisei*).

◁ Halley's Comet, photographed through a telescope from Australia in March 1986.

Halley in close-up

After an eight-month journey across the Solar System, *Giotto* homed in on Halley's Comet in March 1986. It flew to within 372 miles (600 km) of the comet, taking spectacular pictures. They showed the nucleus and spotted fiery jets of gas and dust streaming from it.

The nucleus measured about 9 miles (15 km) long and 4 miles (8 km) across. It twisted and turned slowly as it traveled. The surface was surprisingly dark and rough.

△ A broad tail fans out from the head in April 1986. The comet is now heading away from the Sun.

Halley's nucleus proved to be made up mainly of water ice, along with mineral dust and carbon compounds. It was probably a coating of sooty carbon material that made the surface look so dark. Water vapor was also the main substance in the gas cloud surrounding the nucleus. Carbon monoxide and carbon dioxide were also found, along with formaldehyde. The discovery of formaldehyde was very exciting. It is an organic compound that is also found on Earth. It may be comets carry organic compounds around the Solar System.

△ The European space probe Giotto, which passed only about 372 miles from Halley's comet.

SUN POINTER

◁ *Giotto* spots glowing gas jets spurting out of the comet's dark nucleus.

3443

Catch a Falling Star

Specks of space dust burn up in a flash when they enter the atmosphere.

The space between the planets is full of bits of matter. They may be as small as specks of dust or as large as boulders. Astronomers call these bits of matter **meteoroids**.

Where do meteoroids come from? Some are the little bits left over from the time the Solar System was born, about 4.6 billion years ago. Others are the bits comets leave behind as they travel near the Sun.

The Earth passes through swarms of meteoroids all the time as it travels through space. And those nearby are attracted by the Earth's pull, or gravity.

△ An artist recorded a brilliant fireball in the skies of outer London in February 1850.

They plunge toward the ground, some at speeds of 62,000 miles (100,000 km) an hour or more. As soon as they hit the gases in the Earth's atmosphere, the meteoroids start to heat up because of friction. They get hotter and hotter and start to burn up. As they burn, they leave behind fiery trails. It is these trails that we see in the night sky as meteors, popularly called shooting or falling stars.

Meteoroids big and small

Most of the meteoroid particles that cause meteors are about the size of a grain of sand. They burn up by the time they have reached a height of about 50 miles (80 km) above the Earth, leaving nothing but fine ash behind.

National Geographic explains how planets are made, with help from gravity.

△ Not all streaks in the sky are made by meteors. The spacecraft *Apollo 8* made this one when it returned to Earth after flying around the Moon.

▷ Bright meteors flash through the sky in November 1998 during the Leonid meteor shower.

▽ A large meteor blazes a trail through the sky and heats up so quickly that it explodes. Some bits may survive and fall to the ground.

Light in the zodiac
The dusty particles that fill the space between the planets can cause faint glows in the night sky. This can happen just after the sky darkens in the evening or in the dark sky just before sunrise in the morning. We call these glows the zodiacal light, because they can be seen in the constellations of the zodiac.

But most particles are smaller, even microscopic in size. They do not burn up as meteors but drift slowly through the atmosphere and eventually settle on the ground.

Showers of meteors

On most clear nights, you should be able to see up to about 10 meteors every hour. They can come from any direction and are known as sporadic meteors.

But, at certain times of the year, many more meteors appear than usual, sometimes hundreds an hour. When this happens, we call it a **meteor shower.**

A shower happens when the Earth travels through a stream of particles left behind by a comet. In a shower, the meteors come from the same part of the sky. The shower is named after the star constellation the meteors appear to come from. For example, in August every year, a shower comes from the direction of Perseus, and the meteors are called the Perseids.

Stones from the Sky

Bits of rock and metal from space continually bombard the Earth.

Some of the meteoroids captured by the Earth's **gravity** are much bigger than average. They only partly burn up as they travel through the atmosphere. The bits that are left fall to the ground as **meterorites**.

Thousands of meteorites have been found throughout the world. Most of them are little bigger than pebbles. Only a few really big ones are known. The biggest is one found in Namibia in southwest Africa. It is called the Hoba meteorite and it measures more than 8 feet (2.5 m) across and weighs about 60 tons.

Large meteorites hit the ground so hard that they dig out pits, or **craters**. More than 120 craters are known on the Earth. The largest is Meteor Crater in the Arizona Desert.

▷ Arizona's famous Meteor Crater is the finest on Earth. It measures 4,150 feet (1265 m) across and 575 feet (175 m) deep.

Irons and stones

The Hoba meteorite is made up of metal, like all the large meteorites that have been found. Metal meteorites are known as **irons**, because they are made up of iron, with some nickel. The two metals form a special alloy. When a piece is polished and treated with acid, a fascinating criss-cross pattern shows up.

◁ An iron meteorite found near Meteor Crater. When polished, it shows a typical criss-cross pattern.

Most meteorites are made up of minerals, like the rocks and stones on the Earth. That is why they are called **stones**. The most common types are known as chondrites. They usually contain rounded lumps of silicate minerals (chondrules). Some are rich in carbon compounds.

A much rarer group of meteorites contain both metal and mineral fragments. They seem to be a combination of the other two types, and are called stony-irons.

Meteorites young and old

Scientists have methods of finding out how old meteorites are. Most meteorites turn out to be older than any rocks found on the Earth's surface. They are about 4.6 billion years old. This means that they date back to the time when the Solar System was born.

▷ This meteorite was found buried in ice in Antarctica in 1981. Scientists think it probably came from Mars.

A few meteorites are much younger. Some found in the Antarctic are only about 1.3 billion years old. And scientists now think that these came originally from the planet Mars. They were probably flung into space after a huge asteroid hit the planet. Other **asteroids** may have come from the Moon, as they have a similar makeup to Moon rocks brought back by the Apollo astronauts.

Gaining weight
The Earth gains up to about 80,000 tons in weight every year from the meteorite material that rains down on it from outer space. Most of this material is in the form of tiny particles of space dust and ash (from burning meteors). These particles are known as micrometeorites.

Shaping other Worlds

On the Earth today, we find only a few craters made by meteorites. When the Earth was young, swarms of rocky lumps smashed into our planet. But, over the years, the craters they made have disappeared. They have been worn away by the action of the weather or covered up by upheavals in the Earth's crust.

The rocky swarms also bombarded the other bodies in the Solar System. And most of them still bear the scars of this bombardment.

△ Saturn's Moon Enceladus has only a few craters because its surface is so young.

◁ Our own Moon is covered with thousands of craters. Its surface hasn't changed for billions of years.

A battered face

Meteorites have largely shaped our companion in space, the Moon. Thousands of craters, large and small, cover the surface. The largest ones, such as Bailly and Clavius, are more than 150 miles (250 km) across. They have high walls, which descend in terraces to deep floors. Often there are mountain peaks in the middle of the craters.

Even the huge plains we call seas came about because of meteorite bombardment. Particularly large rocks slammed into the Moon, creating mountainous walls. The force of the impacts caused volcanoes to erupt. The lava they gave off flooded the huge craters, creating the vast flat seas.

Assault on the planets

We can also see the effect meteorites have had on the other rocky planets—Mercury, Venus, and Mars. Mercury is covered with craters all over. They have not worn away over the years because the planet has no atmosphere. And without an atmosphere, it has no weather to wear away the surface. Also, there have been no volcanoes or ground movements to help cover up the old craters.

The next planet out, Venus, has no really old craters, and very few new ones. The reason is that the planet is still very active, like the Earth. Volcanoes are found all over Venus. In recent times they have erupted time and time again, flooding the landscape with lava. Many old craters have been covered up. Venus also has a thick atmosphere, which helps protect it from small meteorites—they burn up before they reach the ground.

Meteorite craters are also found on Mars, but mainly in certain areas. Other areas are flat plains regions, which have been created by erupting volcanoes and maybe by ancient oceans.

△ Phobos, Mars's largest moon, is only about 12 miles across, but it is peppered with craters.

◁ Mercury is the most heavily cratered planet in the Solar System. Few areas have escaped bombardment by meteorites.

The giant planets

Meteorites have had no visible effects on the giant planets beyond Mars—Jupiter, Saturn, Uranus and Neptune. This is because these planets have no solid surface—they are made up mainly of gas and liquid. But most of the solid **moons** of these planets are heavily cratered.

Many Mini-Planets

A swarm of rocky bodies circles the Sun between Mars and Jupiter.

The four rocky planets—Mercury, Venus, Earth and Mars—lie quite close together in the center of the Solar System. Then comes a huge gap of nearly 370 million miles before the next planet, Jupiter.

Astronomers first realized there was a gap when they began calculating planets' orbits around 1600. The German astronomer Johannes Kepler suggested that there ought to be another planet in the gap, but two hundred years went by and no planet was found. Then, on the first day of January 1801, an astronomer from Sicily named Giuseppe Piazzi spotted one. He called it Ceres after the patron goddess of Sicily. It looked like a star and so could not be very big. Soon three other "mini-planets" were discovered in the gap: Pallas (in 1802), Juno (1804), and Vesta (1807).

△ Asteroids show up as streaks in this photograph.

asteroid belt

Jupiter

Asteroid swarms

Since then thousands of mini-planets have been discovered. Astronomers call them **minor planets** or asteroids. Most of the asteroids circle the Sun in a broad band between the orbits of Mars and Jupiter called the asteroid belt. The middle of the belt lies about 250 million miles from the Sun.

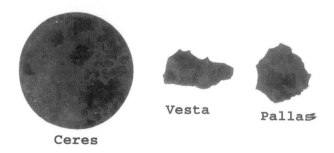

Ceres

Vesta

Pallas

△ Ceres is nearly twice as big as the next largest asteroids, Vesta and Pallas.

The celestial police
In September 1800, a Hungarian nobleman named Baron Franz von Zach decided to organize an international search party for the "missing" planet between Mars and Jupiter. They became known as the celestial police. One of the police, Heinrich Olbers, discovered the second and fourth asteroids, Pallas and Vesta. Another searcher, Karl Harding, discovered the third, Juno.

Not all asteroids stay in the asteroid belt. Some wander as far as the orbit of Saturn, while others wander in towards the Sun. One, called Icarus, gets closer to the Sun than the planet Mercury. Several asteroids wander near the Earth's orbit. They are known as **Near-Earth Objects** or NEOs (see page 30).

The centaur asteroids

As well as the ordinary asteroids, there are other bodies known as the Centaur asteroids. They have been found circling the Sun as far out as the orbit of Neptune. American astronomer Charles Kowal found the first one, Chiron, in 1977. Astronomers have also found similar objects even further away in a remote region called the Kuiper Belt.

Sizing the asteroids

The first asteroid discovered, Ceres, is by far the largest. It measures nearly 1000 kilometres across, making it less than a third the size of the Moon. The next largest asteroids (Pallas and Vesta) are only about half the size of Ceres. And in all there are only 25 asteroids bigger than 125 miles (200 km) across.

Looking at Asteroids

Most asteroids are shapeless lumps, battered by repeated collisions.

Most asteroids are much bigger than comets. But they never come close enough to the Earth to be visible to the naked eye, except for Vesta. This asteroid sometimes becomes bright enough to be visible. But you must know exactly where to look for it in the sky. It shows up as a pinpoint of light, like a distant star.

Studying asteroids

Powerful telescopes can detect thousands of asteroids down to a few miles across. They only reflect a feeble light, but astronomers can tell a lot from it. From tiny changes in an asteroid's brightness, they can tell how fast it is spinning and can estimate the asteroid's shape. Most asteroids appear shapeless. Only the biggest, Ceres, appears to be round like the Moon. Astronomers also get information from the spectrum of an asteroid's light. This is the rainbow-like band of color obtained by passing the light through a prism or similar device. From the spectrum, astronomers can work out what the asteroid is made of.

Different types

Asteroids are made up of three main kinds of substances—rock, carbon, and metal. Astronomers group them into three types—S, C, and M. Most asteroids in the inner part of the asteroid belt are S (silicaceous) types, made up of silicate rock. They tend to be reddish in color. Most asteroids in the outer part of the belt are C (carbonaceous) types, containing large amounts of carbon and carbon compounds. They are dark in color, and some are as black as soot.

△ Many small craters cover asteroid 951, named Gaspra. About 11 miles (18 km) long, it was photographed by the Galileo space probe in 1991.

▷ This photo of Vesta was taken by the Hubble Space Telescope. The different colors show that the surface is made up of different materials.

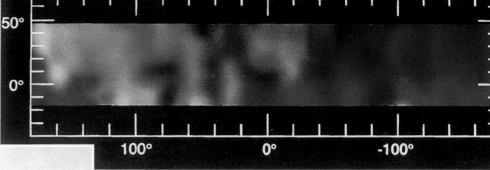

△ Scientists think that this meteorite, found in Western Australia, came from Vesta. It seems to have the same chemical make-up.

The M (metallic) types of asteroids are not so common. They are made up mainly of the metals iron and nickel. Astronomers think that they are probably the centers, or cores, of larger asteroids that were broken apart in collisions.

Asteroids galore
A special telescope called LINEAR, operated by the US Air Force in New Mexico, has spotted an average of more than 1,000 new asteroids every month since it went into operation in March 1998! It has also recorded several hundred NEOs. Originally, LINEAR was set up to track satellites and manmade debris in space.

Asteroid images

No one knew what asteroids looked like until 1991. In that year the space probe *Galileo* sent back pictures of Gaspra. The probe snapped Ida two years later. Both were shapeless lumps of rock, pitted with craters. Since then the Hubble Space Telescope has sent back images of Vesta and other asteroids. Some asteroids have also been imaged from the Earth by using radar.

◁ Asteroid 243, named Ida, which is 34 miles (56 km) long. It has a moon, Dactyl, just 1 mile (1.6 km) across.

Cosmic Collisions

Lumps of rock wandering in space can cause disasters.

In July 1994, astronomers saw something no one had seen before—the bombardment of another world from space. More than 20 pieces of a comet named Shoemaker-Levy 9 crashed into Jupiter, one by one. As they smashed into the planet, great fireballs were created, which astronomers could see in their telescopes.

This event set people wondering. Could something like this happen on the Earth? The answer is, yes, it could. And in the past it has—with terrible consequences.

△ Scientists carefully excavating dinosaur bones. All dinosaurs died out about 65 million years ago.

Death to dinosaurs

About 65 million years ago, over two-thirds of all the plants and animals that lived on the Earth at the time became extinct, or died out. Among them were the "terrible lizards," the dinosaurs. Most scientists now think that this mass extinction happened when the Earth was hit by an asteroid. They reckon that it might have been as big as 9 miles (15 km) across. And they believe that it struck the Earth in what is now the Yucatan Peninsula in Mexico.

△ The fragments of Comet Shoemaker-Levy 9, pictured in May 1994. Two months later, they smashed into Jupiter.

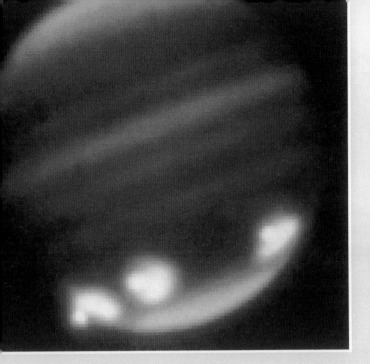

◁ Three massive hot spots show where fragments of Comet Shoemaker-Levy 9 hit Jupiter in July 1994.

Shock waves

Here is what might have happened. The force of the asteroid smashing into the ground dug out a vast crater, hundreds of miles across. Millions of tons of rock were smashed to pieces and blasted into the atmosphere. Shock waves rippled round the Earth. Tidal waves hundreds of feet high sped across the oceans.

So much fine dust was created that it hung in the atmosphere for months. It blotted out the Sun and plunged the Earth into darkness. Most plants died, because plants need sunlight to make their food. And without plants to feed on, most animals died, too, especially big ones like the dinosaurs, which had to eat vast amounts of food to stay alive.

Near misses

In the history of the Earth, 65 million years ago is quite recent. And there is still a chance of asteroids, or comets, hitting the Earth. In 1908, an asteroid or small comet exploded in the atmosphere in Siberia, Russia. The blast felled more than 1,100 square miles (3,000 sq km) of trees in the forest near the Tunguska River. If the explosion had taken place over Moscow, most of the city would have been wiped out.

The Earth-grazers

The asteroids that are the biggest threat to the Earth are the NEOs, or near-Earth objects. There are hundreds of such bodies, and more are being found all the time. In May 1993 a NEO came within 93,000 miles (150,000 km) of our planet—a very near miss indeed.

▷ The forest region in Siberia, Russia, felled by an exploding asteroid or comet in 1908.

The Hubble Telescope

This amazing floating eye in space has given us our best new views of the galaxy . . . and beyond.

Astronomers on Earth peer into the heavens using mighty telescopes. They also search for radio waves and other forms of radiation. But just by being on Earth, they work at a disadvantage. The very atmosphere that keeps them alive also distorts and changes the light and other radiation that shows them what is out there in space. Light passing through the atmosphere, even the thin air atop mountains where telescopes are often placed, will reduce the quality of the pictures they can take. For decades, they knew that the solution would be to have a telescope in space. That was not possible until the 1990s.

Launch . . . and Oops!

Plans for a space telescope were years in the making. Scientists from around the world put together their best ideas. Finally, the US space agency NASA created a plan to build and launch the Hubble Telescope. It would be named for pioneering astronomer Edwin Hubble.

After many years of planning, fundraising, and delays, the mighty telescope was finally put into orbit around the Earth. It blasted off atop a huge rocket and was released into orbit. Almost as soon as its first pictures beamed back to Earth, however, scientists knew they had a problem. The Hubble Telescope had a flawed mirror. This was the single most important piece of the huge machine, which also included almost a dozen cameras, sensors, and measuring devices. But without the perfection of the mirror to bring in the light, they could not see what they wanted to see.

▽ Before and after pictures show the success of the repair job (right).

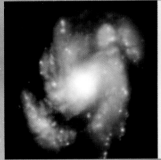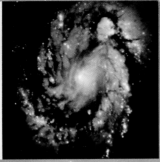

Saved!

A rescue operation was quickly planned and over the course of five Space Shuttle flights, a new mirror was installed and other repairs made. Crews grabbed the telescope, made repairs in the Shuttle's massive storage bay, and then released it back into orbit.

The results were amazing. The view free of distortion from the atmosphere created new and amazing images of deep space. The contrast between the first and second mirror is easily visible in the comparison images shown here.

Edwin Hubble (1889—1953)
This American astronomical pioneer did most of his work at the University of Chicago and the Mount Wilson Observatory in California. He was the first  to show that there were other galaxies beyond the Milky Way and the first to show how far away some of those galaxies are. His ideas about the expansion of the universe revolutionized how we thought of the cosmos.

What we've learned

One of the most important things about the **universe** that the Hubble Telescope has shown scientists deals with how the universe is expanding. Hubble himself (see box) was the first to theorize that things are moving apart. By measuring the changing distances between stars more clearly than ever, the telescope proved his theory and gave a much more accurate measurement of the rate (known as the Hubble constant).

The telescope has also taken images of black holes, traced the crash of a comet into Jupiter, and helped create pictures of nebulae, stars being born, and entire galaxies. The ultimate "eye in the sky" continues to amaze scientists and the rest of us alike.

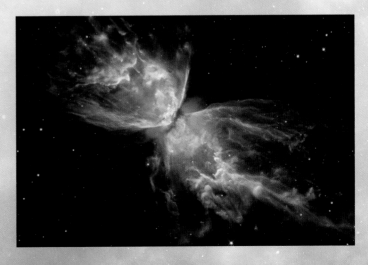

Near-Earth Objects

Earth is surrounded in space by hundreds of objects whizzing by at high speed. Making sure none of them are going to hit us is a full-time job.

Earth orbits the Sun, of course, but we're not the only thing flying through space. Thousands and thousands of objects large and small orbit the Sun. Many of their orbits intersect with Earth or other planets. Over the millennia, collisions between orbiting bodies have happened many, many times. The craters on Earth and the Moon are evidence of that. Some scientists think the Moon itself was created by a large object crashing into Earth. The dinosaurs disappeared after a huge meteor crashed into Earth 65 million years ago.

A similar impact today would cause a worldwide disaster. With all this traffic in a crowded Solar System, scientists around the world keep a close eye on what's out there. They are looking for what they call near-Earth objects (NEOs). If (or when) one of those NEOs is heading to Earth, the worldwide alarm will sound.

Types of NEOs

The two main types of NEOs are asteroids and comets. Asteroids are rocky bodies, usually much smaller than the Moon—some that have come into Earth's vicinity are no bigger than a car. Others,

however, are bigger and they could cause great damage on Earth. Asteroids have a mostly circular orbit around the Sun, staying on a path similar to the planets.

Comets are made of ice, rock, and water. They have much larger, elliptical orbits of much greater length. They come near Earth less frequently, but when they do, they can sometimes be seen ____ ____ th. If they were going to hit Earth, we'd have to do something—fast.

NASA estimates that about 1,000 NEOs are at least .6 miles (1 km) across and 15,000 at least 150 yards (140 m) wide.

How would we stop them?

So the watchers are watching. But what would happen if they found, through examining their photos and data, that one of those asteroids or comets was going to hit Earth? First of all, the chances are incredibly tiny. Even though there are thousands of objects flying around, they're doing so in an enormous space. If you had three marbles and rolled them around a football field, it would be a long time before they connected.

But if a NEO was going to hit, several possible plans might help (and the good news is that we'd have several years' warning). One idea would be to send a spacecraft toward the flying object and detonate a huge bomb nearby it. The nuclear bomb would create a shell of hardened rock as the radiation hit the meteor. That weight would move the orbit just enough to miss Earth. (You don't want the bomb to break up the rock—that might just mean many fragments hitting Earth.) Another plan would be to land on the rock and install a solar sail that would pull the rock into a new orbit. Rockets installed on the rock might do the same thing.

At the moment, there is no need to put such plans in action. But the eyes of the experts are always watching, just in case.

Regular Showers
Every August, star-watchers in the Northern Hemisphere look forward to the Perseid Meteor Shower. For several nights, dozens of streaks of light can be seen in the dark night sky as the meteors hurtle past. They light up as they skirt or enter Earth's atmosphere. They are actually part of the tail of a huge comet, Swift-Tuttle.

The Leonid shower happens in November, as we pass through the tail of another comet.

◁ A huge sail capturing solar winds might move an asteroid off course.

Rosetta: On the Way to a Comet

In 2015, NASA attempted an aeronautical miracle: they tried to land a spacecraft on a moving comet!

Comets fly through the Solar System at amazing speeds. They follow enormously long orbital paths, far wider and longer than planets. Those paths are predictable, however, and with more and more probes being sent out from Earth, the idea of putting a probe onto one of these speeding balls of rock and ice began to take shape. It was an audacious plan. Just getting the probe near to the comet would be like throwing a marble and hoping to hit the Space Shuttle. Science, however, had the answers.

ΔAfter years of planning, *Rosetta* was launched atop this huge rocket.

The plan

In 1986, the space probe *Giotto* (pictured) had been sent out to photograph Halley's Comet, one of the space travelers that comes nearest to Earth. It inspired scientists at the European Space Agency (ESA) to think they could do even more. By 2002, they were aiming their plans at a comet called Wirtanen, but its launch had to be delayed, so they missed their window. They soon found another tar-

get, called Churyumov-Gerasimenko. This comet, first seen in 1969, orbits the sun once every seven years. Scientists at the ESA carefully plotted the path of the comet, calculated how fast their spacecraft would go, and found an intersection point.

In 2004, the ESA finally got *Rosetta* into space. It was launched atop a rocket fired into Earth orbit from French Guiana, on the northern tip of South America.

The long wait

Why did it take so long for the craft to reach the comet? It needed help. The velocity of the rocket leaving Earth with *Rosetta* was enough to get it going toward the comet. But that was not enough force to catch it. By creating an orbital path that took the craft past Mars and then past Jupiter, scientists took advantage of the push of those planets' gravities.

Even then, *Rosetta* would not be going full-out for all those years. From 2011 to early in 2015, the team on Earth put the spacecraft into "hibernation." By using only a minimal amount of energy, it would have enough to do its work once it reached the comet.

On its journey, *Rosetta* passes through mysterious stuff called dark matter—what is that?

▷ *Rosetta* would be powered during its flight by energy captured by solar cells on these outstretched arms.

Why *Rosetta*?

In 1799, French explorers found a large rock fragment in the Egyptian desert. On it were carved three languages: hieroglyphics, demotic (an early form of Egyptian), and Greek. With this stone, for the first time, archaeologists could decipher the picture writing of ancient Egypt, as well as many very old texts. It was like the ultimate codebreaker for historians. The comet probe was given the name, since it would be cracking the comet code for scientists.

The moment of truth

In 2014, *Rosetta* received a signal from Earth to awaken. Its solar panels folded out and began taking in massive energy from the Sun. Its path actually took it in front of the comet's path, so that it was basically waiting for the comet to catch up. As the two paths intersected, *Rosetta* was sent into orbit around the comet, taking thousands of images and video. Its 20-plus instruments started sending back mountains of data from this first-ever close encounter with a comet. Mostly, they were looking for one key piece of information: Was there a safe place to land?

Rosetta Lands!

The successful *Rosetta* landing opened up new windows on comets, orbits, stars, and possibly the origins of the universe.

After traveling more than 4 billion miles (6.4 billion km) since its launch in 2004, *Rosetta* reached the comet Churyumov-Gerasimenko. After using its cameras to help operators find a place to land, *Rosetta* prepared to release the tiny lander, called *Philae*. Back on Earth, controllers in Europe waited for the signal that *Philae* had made it.

▷ **The machine at the bottom left is one of the landing feet of the *Philae*, firmly placed on the surface of a comet!**

Landing Day

The controllers found what they hoped was a flat, soft landing for *Philae*. After maneuvering *Rosetta* into position, they released the lander . . . and crossed their fingers. For more than seven hours, they waited helplessly as the lander slowly moved toward the comet's surface.

Finally, cheers erupted at control stations in France, Germany, Argentina, and around the world: *Philae* had landed!

It was not a clean landing, however. The tiny craft extended its base feet, but instead of settling in . . . it bounced! Photos showed the craft bouncing several times before coming to rest.

Within seconds, it began taking measurements and beaming them back to Earth.

What it found

The first thing *Philae* "told" scientists was that it had detected particles of matter that could be organic—that is, they could be something like living matter. That doesn't mean there are aliens on the comet, but such particles were somewhat unexpected.

While in orbit, *Rosetta* saw jets of gas spewing from the comet's surface, creating winds that were unexpected in a comet. Scientists think those jets are caused when areas of the comet rotate to face the Sun, heating the surface and the ice underneath. That "dumping" of water vapor was much higher than expected.

Other instruments looked at the actual water and found that it was a type of water very much unlike that on Earth.

Philae pumped out these and other discoveries for nearly 60 hours until its batteries wore down. *Rosetta* flew on, perhaps with enough life left to visit asteroids and other bodies.

Philae is still on the comet, a reminder of a great achievement by human beings.

▽ For such a small device, *Philae* is packed with tools. This diagram shows all the different ways that Philae can gather information and images.

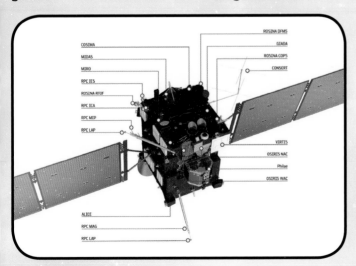

Why it matters

By landing *Philae* onto the comet and investigating the flying rock, scientists are actually looking backward. The theory is that comets were probably created about the same time as the solar system and have change little since. By learning more about comets like Churyumov-Gerasimenko, we may learn more about where we came from. Did comets crashing into a youthful Earth bring important life-creating matter? Did the water vapor spilling from the comet help jump-start Earth's water?

The *Rosetta* mission answered some questions about comets. But it also raised many more. The investigation into these amazing flying objects will continue.

Nothing but the Facts

METEOR SHOWERS

Shower	Constellation	Begins	Ends	Max. number per hour
Quadrantids	Boötes	Jan 1	Jan 6	110
Eta Aquarids	Aquarius	May 2	May 7	20
Delta Aquarids	Aquarius	July 15	Aug 15	35
Perseids	Perseus	July 25	Aug 18	65
Orionids	Orion	Oct 16	Oct 26	30
Leonids	Leo	Nov 15	Nov 19	varies
Geminids	Gemini	Dec 7	Dec 15	55

THE BIGGEST METEORITE CRATERS

Name	Place	When discovered	Diameter (feet/meters)
Meteor Crater	Arizona, USA	1891	4150/1265
Wolf Creek	Australia	1947	2788/850
Henbury	Australia	1937	656/200
Boxhole	Australia	1937	574/175
Odessa	Texas, USA	1921	557/170

THE BIGGEST METEORITES

Name	Type	Weight (tons)	Where found
Hoba West	Iron	60	Near Grootfontein, SW Africa
Ahnighito	Iron	30.5	Cape York, West Greenland
Bacuberito	Iron	27	Mexico
Mbosi	Iron	26	Tanzania, East Africa
Agpalic	Iron	20	Cape York, West Greenland

Meteor notes

WHAT A SHOWER

The number of meteors seen in Leonid meteor showers varies widely. At maximum, hundreds can be seen every minute. Maximum showers tend to occur about every 33 years—there were brilliant showers in 1966 and 1999.

METEORITES ON ICE

One of the best places to find meteorites is on the far southern continent of Antarctica. Scientists have already recovered more than 10,000 specimens from there. One of the richest regions is near the Allan Hills in Victoria Land.

MOON METEORITE

On January 18, 1982, the US geologist John Schutt found a meteorite ALHA81005 in the Allan Hills region. When they examined it closely, it proved to be full of tiny glass spheres, just like rocks brought back from the Moon. So this meteorite had originally come from the Moon.

Comet notes

MANY HAPPY RETURNS

Encke's Comet circles the Sun every 3.3 years, the shortest period of any comet. It was named after the German astronomer Johann Encke, who calculated its orbit and predicted its return in 1822. By 2000, it had been seen on its last 58 returns. It easily beats Halley's Comet, which has been seen on only 28 returns (since 240 BC).

MESSIER'S TABLE

One of the great comet hunters of the 1700s was the French astronomer Charles Messier. Like most astronomers of the day, he was constantly confusing comets, which often look rather like fuzzy patches in the sky, with star clusters and nebulae, which also look like fuzzy patches. So he decided to make a list of nebulae and clusters and note where in the heavens they were to be found. Then he could eliminate them when he was observing. Astronomers still often identify a star cluster or nebula by the number Messier gave it in his list. The Orion Nebula, for example, is referred to as M42.

RECORD BREAKER

Messier was a prolific discoverer of comets, with 13 to his credit. But the record is held by the French astronomer Jean-Louis Pons. By the time he died, in 1837, he had discovered no fewer than 36 comets.

BREAKNECK SPEED

The brilliant comet of 1965, Ikeya-Seki, passed less than 300,000 miles from the Sun. As it approached, the Sun's powerful gravity accelerated the comet until it was traveling at a speed of more than 9.3 million miles an hour. Like most comets that travel so close to the Sun, Ikeya-Seki was broken up by gravitational forces into two or three fragments.

Asteroid notes

LIKE A STAR

In 1802, the German astronomer Heinrich Olbers, a member of the 'celestial police' who were hunting for new planets, turned his telescope on the newly discovered body Ceres, and found another new body in the same part of the sky. He called it Pallas. Astronomers agreed that these objects were not true planets. And the English astronomer William Herschel suggested that they be called asteroids, a word meaning star-like.

MIND THE GAP

In a number of places in the asteroid belt, there are gaps, where no asteroids are to be found. They are called Kirkwood gaps, after the US astronomer Daniel Kirkwood, who predicted their existence in 1857. They occur because of gravitational forces set up by the giant planet Jupiter.

GRAZING THE SUN

The orbit of the asteroid Icarus takes it within 18 million miles of the Sun, within the orbit of the planet Mercury. At close approach, the temperature of its surface must be more than 500°C. It is named after a character in Greek mythology who escaped from captivity by means of wings, held together by wax. But he flew so close to the Sun that the wax melted, and he plunged to his death.

Time Line

65,000,000 BC

A massive asteroid smashes into the Earth, creating dust clouds that blot out the Sun for months. Hundreds of species of plants and animals die out.

50,000 BC

A huge meteorite hits the Arizona desert about this time, digging the Arizona Meteor Crater.

240 BC

The comet we now call Halley's Comet is recorded for the first time.

1066

A comet appears at the Battle of Hastings—another sighting of Halley's Comet.

1682

The English astronomer Edmond Halley suggests that the comet of this year is a regular visitor to Earth's skies and predicts that it will return in 1758.

1758

As Halley predicted, the comet returns and is henceforth named after him.

1801

The Italian astronomer Giuseppe Piazzi discovers the first asteroid, Ceres, on January 1.

1861

The US astronomer Daniel Kirkwood suggests a relationship between meteors and comets.

1908

A comet or asteroid explodes near the Tunguska River, Siberia, laying waste to vast areas of forest.

1950

The Dutch astronomer Jan Oort proposes that a great "cloud" of comets lies at the edge of the Solar System. The US astronomer Fred Whipple suggests that a comet's nucleus is like a "dirty snowball."

1966

The Leonid meteor shower on November 17 is spectacular, with thousands of meteors an hour visible.

1977

The US astronomer Charles Kowal discovers a far-flung asteroid, named Chiron.

1986

Halley's Comet is seen best in the Southern Hemisphere. The *Giotto* probe flies near it on March 14.

1991

The *Galileo* probe takes the first picture of an asteroid, Gaspra.

1993

In May, an asteroid passes within 93,000 miles of the Earth—a near miss.

1994

The many pieces of Comet Shoemaker-Levy 9 crash into Jupiter in July.

1996

Comet Hyakutake makes a spectacular visit to Earth's skies. NASA scientists suggest that a meteorite from Mars (ALH84001) contains microscopic fossils.

1997

Comet Hale-Bopp blazes in spring skies, becoming one of the brightest comets of the century.

1999

Space probe *Deep Space 1* swoops within 15 km of an asteroid named Braille in July.

2000

The NEAR probe goes into orbit around Eros on February 14, beginning a year-long study of the tiny asteroid.

2015

The *Rosetta* spacecraft successfully lands the probe *Philae* on the surface of a comet for the first time.

Words to Understand

asteroids
Small lumps of rock and metal that circle the Sun in a band— the asteroid belt—between the orbits of Mars and Jupiter.

atmosphere
The layer of gases around the Earth or another planet.

axis
An imaginary line through the middle of a spinning body, around which the body spins.

coma
The glowing head of a comet.

comet
A small lump of ice and dust that starts to shine when it gets near the Sun.

constellation
A group of bright stars appearing in the same direction in the sky.

crater
A circular pit in the surface of a planet or moon. Most craters are made by meteorites, but some are the mouths of ancient volcanoes.

dust tail
One of the two tails of a comet, made up of dust, which reflects sunlight.

fireball
An exceptionally bright meteor, which may explode.

gas tail
One of the two tails of a comet, made up of glowing gas.

gravity
The force of attraction that every body has because of its mass.

head
The front part of a comet, properly called the coma.

interplanetary
Between the planets.

irons
Meteorites made up mainly of iron.

meteor
The fiery trail left by a meteoroid burning up in the atmosphere.

meteorite
The remains of a large meteoroid that hits a planet or a moon.

meteoroid
A piece of rock or metal found in space.

meteor shower
A time when more meteors than usual can be seen.

minor planets
Another name for the asteroids.

moons
The common name for a satellite.

Near-Earth Objects (NEOs)
Asteroids that pass close to the Earth.

nucleus
The small solid part of a comet, within the head.

orbit
The path in space one body follows when it circles another.

period
A length of time in a regularly repeating cycle, such as the period of a comet: the time it takes to circle the Sun.

planet
One of the nine bodies in space that circle the Sun.

probe
A spacecraft sent to explore other heavenly bodies, such as planets.

satellite
A small body that orbits around a larger one; a moon. Also the usual term for an artificial satellite, a spacecraft that orbits the Earth.

shooting star
A popular name for a meteor.

solar
To do with the Sun.

Solar System
The Sun and the family of bodies that circle around it, including planets, comets and asteroids.

solar wind
A stream of particles that the Sun gives off.

stones
Meteorites made up mainly of rock.

tail
The part of a comet that streams away from the head.

universe
Space and everything that is in it—galaxies, stars, planets, and energy.

Index

Picture credits
Art Archive: 9b. Mary Evans Picture Library: 16t. Nick James: 17.
Robin Kerrod/Spacecharts: 6, 18-19, 19t. MPIA/Spacecharts: 27t.
Martin Mobberley: 4-5. NASA/Spacecharts: 11t, 16-17, 20, 21, 26b.
Natural History Museum: 18c. NOAO/Spacecharts: 7t, 12-13, 15t.
Novosti/Spacecharts: 27b. Philippe Plailly/Eurelios/SPL: 26c.
RAS/Spacecharts: 7b, 17c, 22b. RGO/Spacecharts: 11b.
RO, Edinburgh/Spacecharts: 14b. Spacecharts: 8-9, 8b, 9t, 12t,
13b, 15c, 15b, 17t, 24, 25. NASA: 28-33.